David Gatward

Adverts and Advent

A rundown through Advent for teenagers

kevin
mayhew

First published in 2002 by
KEVIN MAYHEW LTD
Buxhall, Stowmarket,
Suffolk, IP14 3BW
E-mail: info@kevinmayhewltd.com

© 2002 David Gatward

The right of David Gatward to be identified
as the author of this work has been asserted
by him in accordance with the Copyright, Designs
and Patents Act, 1988.

No part of this publication may be reproduced,
stored in a retrieval system, or transmitted, in
any form or by any means, electronic, mechanical,
photocopying, recording or otherwise, without
the prior written permission of the publisher.

All rights reserved.

Scripture quotations are from the Contemporary
English Version © American Bible Society 1991,
1992, 1995. Used by permission. Anglicisations ©
British and Foreign Bible Society 1996.

9 8 7 6 5 4 3 2 1 0

ISBN 1 84003 955 8
Catalogue No. 1500538

Cover design by Matthew Lockwood
Edited and typeset by Elisabeth Bates
Printed and bound in Great Britain

Contents

Foreword	7
How to use this book	9
1 December – Love your neighbour	11
2 December – Wilderness man	14
3 December – The Word became flesh	16
4 December – Prophets	19
5 December – Follow the leader	22
6 December – Really?	26
7 December – A little bit afraid	29
8 December – News for the shepherds	32
9 December – Not princes or kings	35
10 December – The good and the bad	38
11 December – Rough and simple	41
12 December – Census	44
13 December – Jumping baby	47
14 December – Scared	50
15 December – Mary and Joseph	54
16 December – Mind-blown	57
17 December – Presents	60
18 December – Simplicity	63

19 December – No doubt	66
20 December – Louder than ever	70
21 December – God chose Mary	74
22 December – No room	77
23 December – First witnesses	80
24 December – Christmas Eve	83
25 December – Christmas Day	86
31 December – New Year's Eve	89
1 January – New Year's Day	92

*For Trub, Carol,
Iain and Helen*

Foreword

If you believed the hype, it'd be easy to think that Christmas began in September. Winter holidays are advertised alongside the news. TV becomes nothing more than an excuse to get children to bully their parents into buying them things they don't need that cost too much. The manufacturer of a certain soft drink seems intent on having the world convert to the belief that drinking its main product is not just 'it', but 'life'. Father Christmas isn't bothered about whether you've been good or bad or naughty or nice, just whether you've got a good credit rating and can afford the repayments. And if you thought it was all about peace and goodwill to all men, think again. It's actually about getting what you want, eating what you want, drinking what you want, and watching a selection of repeat films while taking tablets for indigestion.

That's the cynic in us all talking. That bit of us which is getting a bit tired of seeing the Christmas decorations go up that little bit earlier each year, of adverts telling us to forget about Christmas and instead look forward to the Boxing Day sales. That part of us which wishes that it was for once, a bleak midwinter, that the frosty wind was moaning, and that, away in a manger, no crib for his bed, the little Lord Jesus really was laying down his sweet head, and the world was amazed at what it all actually meant.

But that's the trouble with Advent. It's so easy to get caught up in the presents and lights and cartoons that we simply forget what it really is all about. We just drift on through, eating the rubbish chocolates in the calendar, without any thought as to why Jesus was born in a dark, damp and smelly stable, surrounded by animals, his teenage mum and a father who's trade was about as tough as they come. All it takes, though, is a little time.

Sometimes it's nice to have some help. Now I'm not suggesting that in these pages you'll find the answer to rediscovering what this time of year is all about. And it's certainly not some crazy, mad, radical, whizzy study guide full of gimmicks and little else. Hopefully though, as you read through the thoughts, ideas, challenges, prayers and Bible readings for each day, you'll be able to take a fresh look at what this truly great season means to you and your mates, your life, and what you're doing with it.

DAVID GATWARD

How to use this book

Right – first of all, it's not really that difficult. This is a book you can use on your own or with a bunch of mates. Rather than just looking at Advent, I've included New Year's Eve and New Year's Day, just to give you a chance to see what the season means for the new year ahead. What I've tried to do is give you something to think about throughout each day as Christmas draws closer. So there are four bits to each day.

Bible reading - I don't think I really need to explain this bit.

Prayer - a simple prayer to help you think about what the reading's all about.

Questions - a few questions or thoughts on the reading to challenge you and get you thinking, that kind of thing.

Thought - a paragraph or two on what the reading might be getting at, a look at the wider picture and perhaps a few things to annoy you, shock you, get you thinking, questioning, laughing . . .

So when do you do each bit? Simple - that's up to you. This is a book you can use on your own or with a bunch of mates. That's why I've included some questions, which I guess are nothing more than discussion starters. Stuck for conversation? Open this book and have a look!

You can read a different bit throughout the day, starting with the Bible reading and the prayer in the morning, the questions in the afternoon and the thought bit at the end of the day. Or you can pick and choose, miss a day or two or read it in chunks. Whatever you do, the main aim is to get you thinking a little bit deeper about Advent, about what Jesus, being born all those years ago in a tiny place the world hadn't then even heard of, means to you in the here and now.

1 December
Love your neighbour

Romans 13:8-10
Let love be your only debt! If you love others, you have done all that the Law demands. In the Law there are many commands, such as, 'Be faithful in marriage. Do not murder. Do not steal. Do not want what belongs to others.' But all these are summed up in the command that says, 'Love others as much as you love yourself.' No one who loves others will harm them. So love is all that the Law demands.

Lord,
   it's the beginning
   of Advent.
I've got a choice:
   to do nothing with my time
   other than the usual and expected,
   or instead
   to think about what it all means,
   why we celebrate Christmas at all,
   what you being born all those years ago
   means to me in the here and now.

It's not really a difficult choice, Lord,
   but I guess it's going to require me
   to put a little bit more effort in
   than usual.

But it's effort I want to put in, Lord.
I want to explore,
   to learn,
   to question,
   to discover.
Not just at this time of year,
   but throughout my life.

Help me this year, Lord,
   to really look at your birth
   and perhaps
   find my own beliefs
   and faith in you
   given new life.

Amen.

Is there anything you really want to learn, understand or discover during Advent?

What does Advent actually mean to you right here, right now?

Write down as quickly as possible all that you'll be doing this Christmas. Now look at the list and see how much of it has anything to do with what Christmas is really about, and how much of it is to do with the wrapping paper and tinsel and sparkly lights. Is something missing from what you're doing this Christmas?

1 DECEMBER

So, we have 10 commandments, but here we learn that they can all be summed up in one simple phrase: love your neighbour as you love yourself. All the other commandments hinge on this one, and by carrying it out to the letter, all the other commandments should come naturally. It makes sense really. Love someone as you love yourself; in other words, treat others as you yourself would expect and want to be treated. Do this, and doing anything which would harm them is an impossibility. And here we are in Advent, the run-up to Christmas. That time of year when people try to show each other what they really feel about each other. Well, that's what they're supposed to do, according to the hype. But being a Christian adds a lot more to it. This isn't simply an excuse to get very excited about getting something very expensive. It's about looking at how it all started, about how real love in one man came to this world in rather odd circumstances, and how that man changed the world and changed us.

2 DECEMBER

It's just another day, same old role to play, same old stuff to do. Some of it's good, some of it's bad, some of it you forget as soon as it's done. Where's Jesus in it all? If he really is with you right now, then he's with you for the rest of your day, week, month, year, life . . .

Is there any excitement in your eyes about the birth of Jesus? What are you really looking forward to?

A wilderness man. A man who dressed rather unconventionally and ate food that most people would avoid rather than touch, never mind taste. Imagine meeting him – what would your reaction be? There's a wildness in his eyes, he's dirty, worn, but so alive you can't help but listen in to what he's on about. He's talking about something and it sounds just a little bit important. You catch a few words, something about someone coming who sounds rather amazing, someone who'll baptise you with the Holy Spirit. Then he's gone, back into the wilderness, his crazy hair blowing in the wind. But you can't forget that wild look in his eyes or what he was trying to get you to understand.

So here's the question – what does the birth of Jesus actually mean to you? Have you ever thought about it? In a few weeks' time you'll be joining in the celebrations, which are all about saying a big hurrah about Jesus' birth; about getting excited about it, crazy, wild. If that's what it's about, if it really is quite possibly the most amazing thing ever, what are you going to do? How are you going to celebrate? Where's the wildness in your eyes?

3 December
The Word became flesh

John 1:14
The Word became a human being and lived here with us. We saw his true glory, the glory of the only Son of the Father. From him all the kindness and all the truth of God have come down to us.

I'm finding this all rather hard
   to understand,
   comprehend,
   get into my head.
The idea
   that to get to the heart
   of what was going on on earth
   you became one of us.

You were born into our world.
You lived and breathed and walked
   where we walk.
You had friends,
   family.
You experienced thought,
   decision,
   hope,
   despair.

People saw you laugh
   till the tears ran
   and your belly ached.
People saw you cry
   till the tears ran
   and your heart broke.

You lived with us, Lord.
Live with us now.

Amen.

When you do something today, how does it feel to know that Jesus probably did or experienced the same? From the cold of the air on your face to talking and laughing with friends. From being concerned about what was going to happen in the afternoon to just taking some time out. Think about that; the reality of Jesus.

This is exactly what the birth of Jesus into our world is about: the Word becoming flesh and making his dwelling among us. Now John is big on symbolic language. Just read the rest of the book and you'll see what I mean. But here we've got 'the Word' in reference to Jesus. What John's doing is trying to show Jesus as the Word of God, that he is all that God is and does. Check out Genesis and you'll see just how amazing and powerful and creative the Word of God really is. And here we have Jesus born into this world as not only a person, but that Word, that power, that creativity – God's Son. We're presented with this person, this Jesus, who holds such power and yet comes to sit with us around lake Galilee and talk about fish! This person, this Jesus, who met and ate and laughed with people. Who understood them, learned from them and taught them and loved them. The reality of the birth of Jesus is quite an extraordinary thing, isn't it?

4 December
Prophets

Isaiah 9:6-7
A child has been born for us. We have been given a son who will be our ruler. His name will be Wonderful Adviser and Mighty God, Eternal Father and Prince of Peace. His power will never end; peace will last for ever. He will rule David's kingdom and make it grow strong. He will always rule with honesty and justice. The Lord All-Powerful will make certain that all of this is done.

Lord,
    that's a lot of names.
Wonderful Adviser?
Mighty God?
Eternal Father?
Prince of Peace?
That's a lot to live up to, Lord,
    almost too much.

Sometimes,
    if I try to think of all that happened,
    all the goings-on surrounding your birth,
    I feel confused,
    bemused,
    lost.
But these prophecies,

      the idea that people, years before you existed,
         foretold that you'd be turning up?
That's insane, Lord.
And yet there it is,
      in front of me.

Is it any wonder, Lord,
      that I get confused,
      and feel swamped by it all?
Is it any wonder,
      that I spend most days
      asking for you
      to help me understand?

Help me again, Lord.

Amen.

Jesus didn't just turn up at random, say some stuff that made sense, and that was it. This was a birth foretold, a birth that would mean something for the whole of humanity. Amazed yet?

How many of the people you know don't take the birth of Jesus seriously? For how many of them does it have no meaning at all? Ever tried seeing it from their point of view? Step into their shoes for a while, understand why they think the way they do.

4 DECEMBER

Someone asked me an interesting question recently: 'Where have all the prophets gone? Why aren't there any about now?' It's easy to see where the question came from. The Bible is stacked full of prophets. They're everywhere, foretelling this and that and the other. Being chased into the wilderness, beaten up and worse. But now? Where are they? If there were prophets then, why aren't there any now? What's happened?

My only thought about this is that perhaps there will never again be any prophets. Why? Well, perhaps everything came to a head in Jesus. If you think about it, if Jesus is who he says he is, there's very little else, if anything, to prophesy, is there? We've been given all that we need, we've been shown all there is to be shown and we've been told all that we need to learn. Now it's down to us. No more foretelling about what's going to happen, or what we should do, is needed. Jesus pretty much ended all that by giving everyone the chance at a new beginning. From now on it really is down to us to get on with it and put into practice all that we've been told. Not an easy task, is it?

5 December
Follow the leader

John 4:25-26
The woman said, 'I know that the Messiah will come. He is the one we call Christ. When he comes, he will explain everything to us.'

'I am that one,' Jesus told her, 'and I am speaking to you now.'

Lord,
    you were born to a world desperate for a Messiah,
    aching for someone
    to save them.
You came,
    you saved,
    and few still listen.

Today, Lord,
    this is a world desperate to ignore what it all meant,
    why you came.
It is a world
    which doesn't understand why it needs saving,
    or from what.
It is this world I live in, Lord,
    trying to make sense of it all,
    and of you in it.

Sometimes
    I shout and scream and yell
    and yet you still don't answer me.
There are answers I need,
    things I have to know,
    but no answer comes.
I just sit,
    surrounded by a cloud of confusion,
    trying to work out what it all means.

Sometimes
    it doesn't mean anything.
It's stuff I've created
    and I've confused myself.
Other times,
    it's so important
    that the ache I feel inside
    is the desperation in me
    to know everything about you,
    about what you know I can achieve with my life,
    about what my purpose could be
    if only I realised what I was capable of.

But these are things
    I can't learn in a minute, an hour, a day.
These are things
    that only a lifetime can ever begin to allow me
    to get a glimpse of what it's all about.

Help me live that lifetime of discovery, Lord.

Amen.

It seems today that we've got all the answers, and if we haven't, well with a bit more research we'll probably get them. We seem obsessed with removing the mystery and majesty of what we are, where we live. Perhaps we need a little bit more of the 'wow' factor in what we do, see, hear, think, live, eat, achieve, discover . . .

This is the only life you get a chance at. No more chances, no rehearsal, this is it. It's down to you to do what you can with it, to live it, to make it something so completely and utterly surprising to the world that, when it ends, you can say, 'I truly lived . . .' The question is, how are you going to make sure that happens?

We're in a bit of a fix now. Why? Simple(ish). When Jesus turned up, loads of people were thinking, 'It'll be OK – the Messiah is coming!' They didn't know when or how, but they had faith in the idea that at some point in history, in their lifetime or someone else's, the Messiah was going to come along and sort it all out. Now here we are, 2000 years later, in the belief that the Messiah has arrived. That's it – the Lord has come. So why is this a fix? Well, look at the world, look at the way we live. Do we as individuals live as though our Messiah has arrived? Does this world look like it's in any way been sorted out? I think not. You see, the trouble with having a Messiah turn up is that you expect certain things to happen. You expect everything to be OK at last, you expect a great and tremendous leader, you expect . . . the expected. God, though, in his infinite and creative wisdom, turns things upside down. And what we get is something radically different. Someone who leads us by serving us, helping us, standing alongside us. There's no grand and golden throne, no army, no pomp and circumstance. In its place we get unconditional love, unconditional understanding, unconditional sacrifice. What we have to ask ourselves though, is: Are we willing to follow the leader?

6 December
Really?

John 1:7-10
He came to tell about the light and to lead all people to have faith. John wasn't that light. He came only to tell about the light. The true light that shines on everyone was coming into the world. The Word was in the world, but no one knew him, though God had made the world with his Word.

Lord,
    all the signs that Christmas is just round the corner
    have nothing to do
    with what it's all about.
The message of Christmas
    is wrapped up in a present
    that no one's bothered to open.
They're more interested
    in the other more colourful boxes
    sitting under a tree.

The run-up to Christmas
    doesn't seem to be about you any more, Lord.
It's like we get really excited about celebrating a birthday,
    hold a huge party,
    and then completely forget to invite you –
    the very person the party is for.
Just how stupid are we?

Don't answer that, Lord,
   let me think about it for a while.

Lord, everyone's talking
   about what they're getting for Christmas.
Everyone's asking each other
   about how much is being spent on them,
   what TV programmes they're going to watch,
   what parties they're going to.

I haven't heard your birth mentioned once, Lord.
At times I'm tempted to ask
   just what they're celebrating,
   why they want to wish each other a 'happy Christmas'.
After all,
   with the amount of presents some people get,
   it's hard to see how it can be anything but happy.

The reality of what actually happened
   has been replaced
   by the fantasy people would rather believe.
It's got nothing to do with saving a world,
   of liberating a creation.

And now, Lord,
   we need liberating
   from our own creation
   of what we think Christmas really is.

Free us, Lord.

Amen.

How would you feel if all your friends started to celebrate your birthday each year but didn't invite you?

The one thing people hate is having something rammed down their throat, being forced into listening to something, believing something. Do it with Christianity and people get upset. Do it with consumerism, with advertising, with spending money . . . who's really complaining now?

So John turns up, says, 'Oi! World! Someone amazing is coming! No, it's not me, so stop asking. This person is what it's all about. The very 'it' of what the world, what you and me and us and them, can become!' The world turns round and says, 'Oh! Really? That's amazing! When's he coming? What's he going to do? What's – oh, what's that over there? . . .'

The world hasn't changed all that much really. It's a bit older, there are more people (who, incidentally, if they were all stood side by side would fit onto the Isle of Wight!), technology has advanced a fair bit, but in essence it's the same old world. We know what we're capable of, we know we have the means and ability to sort ourselves out, our world, but we don't. We happily go on hoping someone else will do it, not because we've got more important things to worry about, just more entertaining, enjoyable ones. We simply don't recognise what we've got, even when it's staring us in the face.

7 December
A little bit afraid

Romans 15:4
And the Scriptures were written to teach and encourage us by giving us hope.

I'll admit something, Lord,
   I don't understand
   or agree with
   everything in the Bible.
Some of it just doesn't make sense,
   some of it contradicts itself,
   and some of it seems just plain wrong.
So how am I supposed to learn from it?

I sometimes find it hard to understand
   why you came to earth all those years ago
   rather than now.
This world seems to need you more than ever.
It's even more bent on its own self-destruction.
It needs you.
We need you.
I need you.
It just doesn't make sense.
Your birth seems so long ago,
   so far away.

Help me
    to bring it closer to today, Lord.

Amen.

Questions, questions, questions. Are they good or bad? Why do some people think questions weigh them down? How are we to learn, to discover, to progress, if we don't ever question? What questions burn you and keep you searching?

Jesus is a historical figure, not a fictional character. He was born, lived and died on this planet on which you now stand. How does that make you feel?

OK, so what's the biggest problem with getting down to reading the Bible? Boredom? Laziness? Fear? Well, perhaps all these play their part, but there is another – that part in us that likes to question and of which we are just a little bit afraid. After all, questions mean that not everything is easy to understand. Questions lead not just to answers but to more questions. And we need something more solid, something more definite. Questions rock foundations, challenge, move us into places and ideas that perhaps we're not that comfortable with. And they also free us, liberate us from ideas and thoughts and actions and beliefs that don't sit right with what it's actually all about. But then isn't that part of the role of the Bible? And in turn, isn't that part of what Jesus coming to this earth is all about? To free us? To challenge us? To rock foundations? Think about how he turned up on this planet, and from the very beginning of his life, how he instantly challenged the norm, what's accepted, what this world is comfortable with. People wanted a messiah who would arrive in a blaze of glory and swipe down the enemy. Instead they got someone who led by serving, who got involved, who got his hands dirty. Someone who asked questions. Which would you rather follow?

8 December
News for the shepherds

Luke 2:15-16
After the angels had left and gone back to heaven, the shepherds said to each other, 'Let's go to Bethlehem and see what the Lord has told us about.' They hurried off and found Mary and Joseph, and they saw the baby lying on a bed of hay.

Lord,
   we celebrate a birthday
   we've forgotten the meaning of.
Instead
   we just celebrate something easier.
A bit of goodwill here,
   some 'merry Christmas' there,
   and we feel like the world's already a better place.
After all,
   all it really needed
   was some turkey and pudding,
   a few television reruns,
   some gifts no one really needs,
   and a false hope that this year
   it really would snow on Christmas day.

The meaning of Christmas?
We've forgotten it, Lord.

It's in front of us
>   and yet we still can't see it.

I heard a saying once –
>   you can't help someone
>   unless they actually want to be helped.

You've tried to help us, Lord,
>   and you have,
>   but I think perhaps the problem
>   lies with us.

No matter how much you want to help us
>   we just don't want to be helped.

And as Christmas approaches,
>   we take one more step
>   away from what it really is all about.

If only we were more like those shepherds, Lord.
Alive, excited, desperate to tell everyone
>   about what was going on.

If only . . .

Amen.

What's getting you really excited at the moment? Is there something you're looking forward to getting? Is there something you're looking forward to giving?

What's the best bit about presents – giving them or receiving them?

How excited are you about the real meaning of this time of year?

Imagine being one of those shepherds. It's a cold night and you're out with the flock, just like any other night. It's your job, your livelihood. You have to protect the sheep from predators, make sure they're safe, stop them from wandering off. Then the darkness disappears and you're in the presence of angels. Something about the Son of God being born. You can't believe it, but you do believe it, all in the same moment. And then, later that night, you find yourself in a stable, which was probably just a cave with a few animal pens inside. It's cold and it smells, but there's a warmth from the animals and lamp in the corner. There in front of you are two people. One is a young girl, probably about 15 years old. Next to her is a man, hands calloused from his work, eyes filled with life. They both look exhausted, their clothes covered in the dust you only get when you travel for days. And in front of them, in a container used for feeding the animals, lying on some straw and wrapped in cloth, is a baby. He's yelling his head off, breathing those first breaths of life, eyes wide to a new world. And you remember the words of the angel, that this is the Son of God; a baby, born to real people in a corner of the world. And you're amazed.

9 December
Not princes or kings

Luke 2:17-18
When the shepherds saw Jesus, they told his parents what the angel had said about him. Everyone listened and was surprised.

It's not what people expected,
   is it, Lord?
Dreams and prophecies
   of the coming of the Messiah
   and the people who are told,
   the people who hear what's going on
   are nothing more
   and nothing less
   than shepherds.

Real people, Lord,
   earth people.
People with real lives
   and real laughter.
People who worked to live,
   who knew poverty and pain
   and love and wonder.

They weren't kings, Lord,
   or politicians

or people of power.
They were ordinary,
    everyday,
    living-their-lives
    people.

These people, Lord,
    these ones who were told
    of what was going on
    in a stable somewhere,
    were the very people
    you came to meet with,
    to eat with,
    to live with,
    to serve,
    to save.

Amen.

Do you find yourself getting bored with the story of Christmas? Why do you think this might be so?

How are you going to make yourself get buzzed about what actually happened?

How would you have reacted to what the shepherds had seen, what they told you they'd experienced? Would it be any different to how you'd react now?

9 DECEMBER

Those shepherds were not the princes and kings you'd expect to be graced with the news of the birth of the son of God. They were normal people with hard lives. They knew all about hardship, about living a life that demanded their all. They were real people, small people, people whose lives were ordinary. Yet in an instant, their ordinary became extraordinary. And these were people who probably didn't scare that easily. After all, if you're a shepherd, protecting your flock is all part of the deal. And that means you versus bears and wolves and whatever else wants to come and chomp on your life's work. So seeing an angel wasn't something they were about to make up. And with the news they were given, with the amazing things they'd seen fresh in their minds, all they could do was tell others, which must have been quite a sight to behold. These men, down from the hills, hardened and tough and wild, telling people about a baby, about angels, about the son of God being born. How would you react to the news? How do you react now?

10 December
The good and the bad

Psalm 42:8
Every day, you are kind, and at night you give me a song as my prayer to you, the living Lord God.

Lord,
    apparently 'tis the season to be jolly',
    and I should be singing,
    'fa la la la la, la la la la'.
Well, I'm not,
    my heart's just not in it.
I'm not interested in all the happiness
    and fun I'm supposed to be having.
It doesn't feel right,
    it doesn't feel true.

I don't quite know what's wrong, really.
Only a few days to go
    and it'll be holidays
    and then presents
    and lots of fun with the people I love.
But right now,
    right here where I am,
    I've lost that 'yuletide cheer'
    and don't seem to be able
    to find it again.

Thing is though, I'm still looking forward to it all.
I may be low,
    but I'm still excited,
    and I'm lucky because of it.
I caught one of those charity adverts on TV, today.
Perhaps that's why I'm down.
I was just struck with the thought
    of what it must be like
    to dread Christmas.
Of what it must be like
    to wish the season away
    as quickly as possible.

Lord,
    as I buck myself up
    and get into the spirit of things again,
    help me to remember those
    for whom this season is less than jolly.
Because behind all the tinsel
    there are people trying to survive
    through another season of cold,
    loneliness and fear.

Amen.

So, for whom do you think Christmas isn't a great time of year?

What could you do to help those in need over the next few weeks?

What is your church, your youth group, doing to take the message of Christmas to the people who really need to experience it?

Life isn't all smiles and laughter. Quite the opposite sometimes. And at those times, when everything really is awful, it's easy to agree with the sentiment, 'I wish it could be Christmas every day . . .' If only every day involved great surprises, everyone smiling and joking and being together and having a great time and giving each other presents and . . . but it's not really very realistic, is it? And would it really be that great if all of life was like that? Isn't half the fun of relaxing knowing that you've earned it? Isn't the sound of laughter even more good for the soul when it takes away those feelings that are getting you down, turning your dark day just that bit lighter? Isn't getting somewhere is life all the more worthwhile if you actually have to do something to get there, rather than just coast along and end up anywhere? Isn't going through the good and the bad, the easy and the tough, all the time doing our all to hold onto the hand of God, the very thing that shapes who and what we are, what we're about, what we're capable of, what we can give back to the world, to God?

11 December
Rough and simple

Hebrews 2:17-18
He had to be one of us, so that he could serve God as our merciful and faithful high priest and sacrifice himself for the forgiveness of our sins. And now that Jesus has suffered and was tempted, he can help anyone else who is tempted.

What made you do it, Lord?
What made you come down
   and go through with it?
Did you feel out of touch?
Was it that you didn't understand us any more?
Was the gap between us growing too large?

Or were we out of touch, soon to be out of reach?
Was it that we didn't understand you any more?
Were we making the gap larger by the minute?

Whatever the reason,
   your coming to walk among us,
   to live with us and eat with us,
   to join in our lives with us,
   was something so shocking,
   so amazing,
   so out of the ordinary,

>   that all I can do is sit,
>   amazed.
>   At what you are,
>   what you did,
>   why you did it,
>   and what you're doing now.

Amazed, Lord.

Amen.

Have you ever really thought about why Jesus actually came to earth? The wider picture of his time on earth?

Have you ever really thought that Jesus, that amazing person, walked this very same earth, looked at those very same stars on nights cold enough to freeze your breath?

It's not your average, everyday, run of the mill, birth. On the one hand, you'd expect the Son of God to be born into something grand, a life of power as we see it, of kings and queens and kingdoms. But almost instantly all our preconceptions are turned on their head and we're thrown into confusion. Where is the grandeur we'd usually expect of such a birth? What, no palace? This is a birth which is both rough and simple. It was God born into the heart of what was going on. It was God born into the lives of the people he loved. It was God living with us, being like us in every way, to understand us, experience what we experience and help us. Amazing.

12 December
Census

Luke 2:1-4
About that time Emperor Augustus gave orders for the names of all the people to be listed in record books. These first records were made when Quirinius was governor of Syria. Everyone had to go to their own home town to be listed. So Joseph had to leave Nazareth in Galilee and go to Bethlehem in Judea. Long ago Bethlehem had been King David's home town, and Joseph went there because he was from David's family.

From the very outset, Lord,
    it seems as though your life
    was destined to be a tough one.
There's Joseph and Mary
    with you on the way
    and they've got to uproot,
    get on the road
    and tramp for miles,
    all for a census.

It was a sign of things to come really, wasn't it?
On the road,
    always travelling,
    rarely resting.
Not an easy life, Lord.

12 DECEMBER

Makes me wonder, sometimes,
    about the bits I don't know about.
What happened in those years
    when you were growing, Lord?
How did you find being a teenager?
As awful and crazy as everyone else?
And when you made your way
    through your twenties
    did you find yourself
    constantly questioning,
    trying to work out
    where your life was going?

Sorry, Lord,
    just questions.
There's a lot about you I don't know,
    and some that I think I do.
Help me understand you,
    what you were about,
    what your life meant,
    just a little bit more
    each day.

Amen.

What does the world generally see as the main reason for Christmas?

What's most important to you at this time of year?

Jesus' ministry lasted for three years. That's pretty much all we know about him. Not much really, is it? Wouldn't it be great to know just a little bit of what his life was like before his ministry started? Imagine being able to have a glimpse at his childhood, to read stories by people who watched him grow. Did he get into trouble? What was his favourite game? What were his friends like? What did he have to say about his life even then? Then think about him as a teenager. Was he as troubled as the rest of us, or calm and collected? And in his 20s, did he begin to understand where his life was going, what it was all about? Or was that something he just always knew? Did he grow up knowing what he had to do, what his life would be about, what he would do with it, the power he had? Jesus presents each and everyone of us with so many answers that we sometimes forget the questions he throws into our lives. Not just about his own existence but our own too. Questions, though, aren't a problem. They're not an enormous question mark weighing us down. Instead, they give us that urge to seek and find, to discover, to think, to challenge. Jesus frees us. Questions free us. Perhaps sometimes we forget how valuble that freedom is and what we can do with it.

13 December
Jumping baby

Luke 1:44-45
As soon as I heard your greeting, my baby became happy and moved within me. The Lord has blessed you because you believed that he will keep his promise.

Mary said, 'With all my heart I praise the Lord, and I am glad because of God my Saviour. He cares for me, his humble servant. From now on, all people will say God has blessed me. God All-Powerful has done great things for me, and his name is holy.'

That's some news, Lord –
    to make a baby in a womb jump!
Makes me wonder
    why today
    the news of what happened then
    doesn't seem to have the same effect.

We get excited
    about what we might get,
    the time off,
    the parties,
    the chance to just relax
    and be with people we love,
    the chocolate,
    the enormous dinner . . .

14 December
Scared

1 Corinthians 4:1-5
Think of us as servants of Christ who have been given the work of explaining God's mysterious ways. And since our first duty is to be faithful to the one we work for, it doesn't matter if I am judged by you or even by a court of law. In fact, I don't judge myself. I don't know of anything against me, but that doesn't prove that I am right. The Lord is my judge. So don't judge anyone until the Lord returns. He will show what is hidden in the dark and what is in everyone's heart. Then God will be the one who praises each of us.

Lord,
    when I think about your birth,
    about what it really means to me
    as someone who believes in you,
    has faith in you,
    I find it hard to smile and to celebrate
    and instead I am scared.

I am scared, Lord,
    because of the reality of what it all must mean.
Your birth,
    life,

14 DECEMBER

    death,
    resurrection,
    were so amazing,
    that I just have to take notice.
I have no choice,
    no matter how many doubts
    fill my mind.
I have to look at what you did,
    to listen to your words,
    and then look at my own life
    and think, 'Well? What now?'

It's scary, Lord,
    because the implications are enormous.
The Son of God,
    my God,
    born into this world,
    to teach us,
    show us,
    help us to understand each other,
    and our God.
To lead us back to what it's really all about.

You came to this world
    to save us from ourselves.
You came to show us what love really was about.
And sometimes,
    that truth is scary,
    but then perhaps we need to be scared,
    so that we actually wake up

and listen to what you were trying to get us
to understand.

Scare me, Lord,
and help me to understand you again.

Amen.

What really frightens you about life?

Life is both scary and astounding, the two almost go hand-in-hand. There's an element of risk involved. How does it make you feel when you think of what might happen in your life?

Do you ever wonder what'll happen to the world in your lifetime? Do you ever wonder what you can do to make sure more of the good things and less of the bad things will happen?

Christmas? Scary? What? That can't be possible, can it? Not when it's so full of children and smiles and happiness and Victorian snow scenes and . . . hang on! That's not Christmas! Or is it? Well, take a look around you and what do you see? Is there much evidence of the reality, the frightening truth about the Son of God actually being born? No? Well, just think about it for a moment. Jesus was someone you could walk up to, talk to, tell jokes to. If it was a cold morning you'd have been able to see his breath condense in the air. If you'd have shaken his hand, you'd have felt the hard skin on his fingers. This was a man, a real person, someone with a fire in his eyes, a passion for life. This man was and is the Son of God. Scared yet? Think about it.

15 December
Mary and Joseph

Luke 1:46-49
Mary said, 'With all my heart I praise the Lord, and I am glad because of God my Saviour. He cares for me, his humble servant. From now on, all people will say God has blessed me. God All-Powerful has done great things for me, and his name is holy.'

What must that have been like, Lord –
   to be Mary
   and to feel a baby moving inside her,
   and all the time to hear the echo
   of the words
     she'd heard about who you were,
     what you were,
     what you would do?

How did she stay sane?
How did she cope with her everyday?
This child of hers
   was God's Son.
She'd been chosen
   and was now mother to someone so amazing,
   so world-alteringly powerful,
     that the mind couldn't even comprehend it.

What was she like, Lord,
   as a mother?
Was she strict?
Did she have a really great sense of humour?
Did her eyes sparkle with mischief?
Did she teach you games?
So many questions, Lord!
My life seems so full of them.

Lord,
   there's something reassuring
   about you having lived like us.
To know that you had a mother,
   that you grew up with us,
   got involved with us,
   learned with us . . .

You understand me
   better than I will ever understand myself.
How could I ever follow anyone else?

Amen.

What have been the main points in your life so far?

What experiences have helped to shape you and make you what you are?

How much of your parents, your family, your friends, has

helped to form your character, what you think, what you do, how you act, what you believe?

There's a lot of Mary in Jesus. There's also a lot of Joseph in Jesus. That's probably got quite a lot to do with why they were chosen by God. They weren't just picked at random because the job had to be done by someone. They were chosen because the job couldn't be done by just anyone.

An amazing thought, isn't it? Try to imagine what they were actually like as people. These were people who taught Jesus, introduced him to his first bath, taught him to eat, to walk, to talk. They helped him deal with growing up, with the scrapes of childhood and the heartache of surviving the teens. They cut his hair, laughed with him, cried with him and for him, disciplined him. They sorted him out when he was ill, put him to bed, watched him play with his friends and grow with them. Joseph taught him a trade, showed him how to fetch the wood from the hills, split it, carve it, create with it, use it. They were with him through all those moments, all those decisions and questions and discussions that we just don't know about. The private life of Jesus. We need to remember that Jesus wasn't just that person we hear of in the Bible, but was a person with a life, with friends, with parents that we just haven't been told about. But they were real, his life was real. And when you realise that, it seems even more amazing, doesn't it?

December 16
Mind-blown

Hebrews 2:17-18
He had to be one of us, so that he could serve God as our merciful and faithful high priest and sacrifice himself for the forgiveness of our sins. And now that Jesus has suffered and was tempted, he can help anyone else who is tempted.

Sometimes, Lord,
    I just can't deal with it.
The idea that you were actually God's Son,
    that you did those miracles,
    said those words.
My mind can't take it in;
    it seems too much to handle.

The reality of who and what you are
    is a scary and amazing thing
    all at once.
It doesn't make sense
    and yet it does.

Take the universe, for example.
I stand staring into the night sky.
I see thousands of millions of stars
    and I know that these are only a small part

of what's really out there.
I know that those lights are coming from stars
    which may not even exist any more.
I know that the universe is expanding,
    but I can't help but ask, 'In what?'
I know all this,
    and none of it makes sense,
    it's all too much to comprehend,
    yet I know it's true
    and I still stand amazed
    by the vision in front of me.

Like you, Lord.
If I try to think hard about you being God's Son,
    about the creation of this world,
    about there being a heaven,
    it's all too much.
It seems impossible,
    but yet I know deep down that there's something in it,
    something that clicks
    and I still stand amazed
    by the vision in front of me:
    the vision of you.

Amen.

Does the thought of what Jesus was and is sometimes scare you a bit? Is that a good thing or a bad thing? or both?

What do you see when you look deep into space when the sky is clear?

How do you feel if some of your questions just can't be answered? Does it mean you stop searching?

What, the same Bible passage twice? Why? Well, read it again and see if you can work it out. No? Well, how about this: first time we focused on how this wasn't the kind of birth you'd expect for the Son of God. This time though, think about this, the reality of it. Jesus was God made flesh, human, us. Jesus was both human and God. Mind-blown yet? It was as though a huge chasm between us and God had been bridged. As though God had said, 'That's it, I've had enough! If you're not going to listen then I guess the only way to show you what I mean is to get down there among you, as one of you, and help you to see that it not only makes sense, but it is actually possible!' So Jesus is born, just like you, just like me, except for the obvious differences. And in that moment, as that first-born cry yelled out into the cold air of that night, that connection was made. God who created us, became one of us. Is the wonder of Christmas beginning to sink in yet?

17 December
Presents

John 4:10
Jesus answered, 'You don't know what God wants to give you, and you don't know who is asking you for a drink. If you did, you would ask me for the water that gives life.'

For ever, Lord.
What's it like?
What's it about?
Promises of eternal life,
   of living water.
In my everyday world
   these things don't sit right,
   they don't fit.

It doesn't make sense, Lord.
How can anything last for ever?
How can I live forever?
How can any of what you say
   really be true?
What guarantee is there?

That's the trouble with today, Lord:
   guarantees,
     the thirst for proof.
If you can't see it
   then it probably isn't real.

But deep down,
    that answer's just not good enough.
It seems even more ludicrous
    than the other options.
So which am I to follow?
What am I to believe?

Lord,
    these doubts in my mind
    never fade.
They're always there,
    niggling away.
But neither do I ever seem to lose sight
    of my beliefs,
    of you.

In my doubt, Lord,
    even there
        I find you.

Amen.

How do you go about choosing presents for people? What are the main things you think about when getting someone a present?

How do you feel when you open a present?

Are there any presents you've been given that have really meant something to you?

We give presents for what reasons? To show people we care? To say 'I love you'? To get a present back from that person? To show off how much money we have? To keep up with the Joneses? A lot of the presents we give and get aren't things that last for ever. They're either fun or useful or entertaining, but rarely do we give or receive something that radically changes our lives. Over the years some presents break or get lost or fade or run out. Others become treasured possessions which we keep safe, sometimes hiding them away. It's amazing how a thing can come to mean so much, isn't it? But then we attach so much else to objects in our lives. We burden them with memories and emotions to the point where sometimes it becomes painful to even look at the item, whatever it is. Perhaps that's one reason why things aren't that important after all? What use is something that we use to represent memories which we probably don't need any more? Are there not better things we can do with our minds, our lives, than to live in the past and to use objects to keep us there? And perhaps that's why Jesus wanted to give something more than just a glass of water to quench our thirst. Something that would sustain us for an eternity, no matter what our lives threw at us. Now that's a gift worth receiving. The question is, how well do you know the giver of the best gift ever?

18 December
Simplicity

Galatians 3:22-28
But the Scriptures say that sin controls everyone, so that God's promises will be for anyone who has faith in Jesus Christ. The Law controlled us and kept us under its power until the time came when we would have faith. In fact, the Law was our teacher. It was supposed to teach us until we had faith and were acceptable to God. But once a person has learnt to have faith, there is no more need to have the Law as a teacher. All of you are God's children because of your faith in Christ Jesus. And when you were baptised, it was as though you had put on Christ in the same way that you put on new clothes. Faith in Christ Jesus is what makes each of you equal with each other, whether you are a Jew or a Greek, a slave or a free person, a man or a woman.

Your birth is quite something, Lord.
One event,
   one moment in history,
   that changed everything
   for ever.
Did you ever think you'd have such an impact?
Did you ever think what you'd said
   would pass through generations
   to meet me here,
   today?

It's almost impossible to believe
    that you had something so infectious,
    so original,
    so dynamic,
    that what you taught
    spread like wildfire.
And like the tables in the temple
    your words threw over tables everywhere, Lord.

Everything about you
    saved people
    and enraged them.
It challenged them
    and angered them.
But that's what you get when you preach real freedom.
Some people don't like to hear a bit of hard truth
    about the way they live their lives
    and they retaliate.
    But nothing stopped it spreading, Lord.
Once your word was out,
    that was it,
    and here I am, years later,
    trying to figure out what it all means,
    as our celebration of your birth,
    your arrival,
    draws ever closer.

Amen.

Are there tables in your life which could do with turning over?

How is the radical message brought to us by Jesus going to affect the way you live?

What do you think real freedom is?

Isn't it odd how something started by that man so long ago, how those words he said, those things he did, could have had such an impact? He came from nowhere into a world where there was no such thing as mass communication. It was down to him and his life and the people he infected with what he was trying to show them. The simplicity of the message though still doesn't seem to have hit home. 'Love one another,' he said, 'as you love yourselves.' It can't be put any simpler. Treat someone how you would want to be treated. Do that, and literally everything else falls into place. Yet all you've got to do is take a glance through history, a glance through our news today, and it's almost impossible to believe that a message of such simple beauty could have been so misused, so abused. Followers of Christ have too often been anything but loving. Lives have been lost over so many things that just don't matter. Religion has been used to batter people, to control them, abuse them, destroy them. Yet nowhere is any of this in Jesus' words. How then can we today continue to let the simplicity of what Jesus said, the true life-changing message he brought to us, be abused anymore? What are you going to do about it?

19 December
No doubt

Mark 1:1
This is the good news about Jesus Christ, the Son of God.

John 1:14
The Word became a human being and lived here among us. We saw his true glory, the glory of the only Son of the Father. From him all the kindness and all the truth of God have come down to us.

There's no doubt
    who the writers of the Gospels
    believed you to be.
The Son of God.
The One and Only.
No messing with that really, is there?

Thing is, Lord,
    that nowadays
    all that happened when you were alive
    is so long ago.
We've become detached from it,
    distant.
It doesn't really feel like it can affect us.
And after all,
    isn't it just a nice story
    to keep children amused at Christmas?

Well, it's not really a nice story, is it?
It's a story of excitement,
   danger,
   death,
   resurrection.
It's a story that smacks you round the face
   and makes you sit up and think.
It's a story that enrages some
   and breaks others.
It's a story that here and now,
   I stand in awe of.

Today, Lord,
   something's clicked.
Briefly, it all seems to make sense.
I don't know why,
   I don't know how.
I have no reasons,
   no explanations.
All I know
   is how I feel at this moment in time
   in the presence of the One
   who was born so many lifetimes ago.

I believe in you, Lord,
   and in you in me.

Amen.

Is there anything that you totally and utterly, without a doubt, believe in?

Does doubt scare you? What do you do when you doubt – ignore it or deal with it and try to search for an answer?

Have you ever experienced a moment in your life where, just briefly, everything made sense? What was it like?

The details of Jesus' birth are not found in the Gospel of Mark or the Gospel of John, yet from the outset there's no doubt in anyone's mind as to who they thought Jesus was: the Son of God, the Word became flesh, who came from the Father, full of grace and truth. Their colours are nailed to the flagpole from the word go. Does this matter, though? Does this bring into question all the details of Jesus' birth? Should we perhaps think that it was just made up, that none of it is true? Was some of it written to fit in with some of the Old Testament prophecies?

Sometimes, we get hung up on questions that don't really matter as much as we want them too. The four Gospels are four different accounts of the life of one man who changed the world. Some of the details are different, but then think of the people who know you. Odds are that they all remember different things about you, know you in different ways, have heard different stories about you. Ask them to write about you and some of the stories would be different, some wouldn't add up, some would contradict others, but it wouldn't mean you didn't exist.

The exact opposite in fact! What we do know is that this singular birth changed the world for ever, altered history, changed lives. We were shown in the brief years Jesus walked this earth, that there is a way to live that makes sense, that gives us a new understanding of what being alive is about. That one birth, that one life, and the world was never the same again.

20 December
Louder than ever

Philippians 4:4-7
Always be glad because of the Lord! I will say it again: be glad. Always be gentle with others. The Lord will soon be here. Don't worry about anything, but pray about everything. With thankful hearts offer up your prayers and requests to God. Then, because you belong to Christ Jesus, God will bless you with peace that no one can completely understand.

I want my life to be obvious, Lord.
I want people to look at me
   and see you.
I want people to be able to know
   that I'm one of your followers.
Trouble is, though,
   I don't think it happens very often.

I look at myself
   and can't help but feel that I'm no different,
   that I don't do anything all that special,
   that nothing I say or do
     is that different to what anyone else says or does.
It's as if I'm full of good intentions
   but when push comes to shove
   I'm just a face in a crowd.

20 DECEMBER

I know it's not right, Lord.
I know that this is not what you call me to be
   or want me to be.
And at this time of year more than any,
   people should be able to see me and think,
   'Wow! This really means something to him!
   I wonder why . . .'

My life should get people asking questions.
It should challenge them,
   make them think.
That's real purpose,
   a real life worth living.

Help me, Lord.
I want to stand out in the crowd.
I want to go against the flow.
I want to be different because of you.
I want to be
   what you want me to be, Lord.
That's all there is to it.
No arguing,
   no questions,
     just that.

Help me become
   all that you know
     I'm capable of becoming.

Amen.

Does your life challenge others? Is it a loud life that shouts, 'Hey! Jesus is where it's at!'?

Do you know anyone who has a life you really admire, who makes you sit up and think?

What's missing from the way you live your life? What's wrong with what you're doing? What could you change about you and really start to make a difference?

The reality of the birth of Jesus, of his life, death and resurrection, is something we should be yelling about through every moment of our lives. And at this time of year, our lives should be louder than ever. This isn't just a time to think about Jesus being born. This is a time to get wild about what it all really means to you, to the world. That birth started something. That child, screaming the night away in a cold, damp stable, was a match that lit a fire unlike any fire the world has ever seen before or since. And it's not like he had a group of powerful, educated people to get his message across to the masses. Instead, he chose normal people, people who really knew what it meant to work for a living. People who had hard lives. Some were generally classed as society's scum; tax collectors, prostitutes. But these were the people Jesus met with, made friends with, lit in an instant with a fire no one could put out. It was these people who spread the message of what they'd heard wherever they were. Not just by standing on street corners and yelling, 'God's amazing!' but by living lives according to what Jesus had shown and told them. How loud is your life at this moment? Can people hear Jesus when they see you awake to the day?

21 December
God chose Mary

Matthew 1:23
A virgin will have a baby boy and he will be called Immanuel, which means 'God is with us'.

I've never thought about it like this, Lord.
The huge responsibility
    that Mary took on,
        being your mother.

How did she cope with it?
How did she deal with knowing that growing inside her
    was God's own Son?
It's mindblowing to even imagine it!

She must've been quite a person, Lord.
I wonder how much of her
    we see in Jesus?
I know there's a lot of my mum in me.
Some of the things I say,
    the way I do things,
    what I think about certain things.

At times, Lord,
    are we hearing Mary in your words?
And what of Joseph;

what did he teach you?
What was life like with him?

There are no answers to these questions, Lord,
    but asking them
    seems to make the whole story of you and what you did
    so much more alive,
    so much more real.

Amen.

Have you ever wondered what Mary and Joseph were really like? About what they taught Jesus, about how they brought him up?

If you could meet them, what questions would you have for them? What would you want to know?

God did not force Mary to become the mother of Jesus. It wasn't a blackmail situation. Mary could just as easily have said no to the whole deal and called it off. God respects our freedom – he gave it to us after all. But then I guess God wouldn't have chosen Mary if there was any chance that the answer would have been anything other than a fully committed yes. And Mary's role was an important one. This was someone charged with the duty and responsibility of bringing Jesus into the world, of watching him grow, teaching him, helping him, disciplining him.

God chose Mary perhaps because she was the only woman in the whole of history capable of being the parent God wanted to bring up his Son. Quite a thought, isn't it? This one woman, or if you want to be more accurate, this one girl, was someone God knew was right for this, the most important of jobs. We forget that Jesus had a life before he really started to change the world. He had a childhood, lived through the ups and downs of being a teenager, had his 21st, lived through his 20s. And it was this life where Mary's influence, Mary's life, was a part of what Jesus became. Perhaps Jesus could have only been born to Mary because she was the only woman who could help him become everything that God wanted and knew he could become. Extraordinary, isn't it?

22 December
No room

Luke 2:6-7
And while they were there, she gave birth to her firstborn son. She dressed him in baby clothes and laid him on a bed of hay, because there was no room for them in the inn.

No room, Lord.
Even in the moments before you were born
    your life was different.
After such a long journey,
    all that way to get to a home town
    and then not to be made welcome.
What must that have been like?

Mary, exhausted, probably wanted to just sleep
    and to never wake up.
Joseph, too tired to be as angry as he felt,
    had no choice but to take care of her
    and find her somewhere safe,
    somewhere out of the night
    to give birth.

Not a perfect situation, Lord,
    for the birth of the perfect solution
    to our problems.

It's hard to believe that from such a beginning
   unfolded a story,
   a life,
   that would crack history.

Perhaps you can do the same to me, Lord?
As I think about your birth,
   your arrival,
   perhaps you can be the perfect solution
   to where I'm going wrong,
   and cause such a crack in my own history
   that I'll have no choice
   but to always wear the scar
   with pride?

Amen.

Ever thought about what effect you could have on this world in your lifetime? What kind of crack in history do you want to make?

Where are the scars of Jesus' affect on your life? Are they visible or do you keep them hidden? What are they?

Here's something to get you thinking ... A better translation for 'inn' would actually be 'guest room'. Now guest rooms are generally something belonging to a friend or family. A room in their house that guests can stay in. So we've got Mary and Joseph turning up after their long journey. They've travelled for days, they're exhausted, hungry, desperate to lie down and sleep. And Mary is close to giving birth, wondering just how soon she'll be going into labour. The journey is because of a census, so off they'd tramped days ago to get to Joseph's home town. They arrive and rather than a welcome find that they can't stay in the guest room. Whose guest room though? After all, this was Joseph's home so the odds were that he knew people there, had family. Were they not expecting him and Mary? Why then did they end up lying Jesus in a manger, which implies that they ended up in a stable? What was going on? Even in birth, Jesus found himself alongside people cast out and ignored by respectable society.

23 December
First witnesses

Luke 2:15-18
After the angels had left and gone back to heaven, the shepherds said to each other, 'Let's go to Bethlehem and see what the Lord has told us about.' They hurried off and found Mary and Joseph, and they saw the baby lying on a bed of hay. When the shepherds saw Jesus, they told his parents what the angel had said about him. Everyone listened and was surprised.

That's some news, Lord.
But not only that,
    it's news presented
    by a rather unique messenger!
It's no wonder the shepherds did something about it
    and ran to see what the fuss was all about.

The Bible's an amazing book, Lord,
    but sometimes
    I think it just gives us the bare bones of the story,
    and the emotion,
    the action,
    is missing.

I can't really see the shepherds being so matter of fact
    in the face of such a situation.
They'd have gone wild!

As I try to think about what it must've been like
    to be out in the fields
    and be met by heavenly messengers
    with news of your birth,
    I can't even begin to imagine
    what it was like.
Shock,
    excitement,
    wonder,
    fear,
    confusion . . .
So many emotions.

Lord,
    when I think about your birth,
    I feel something similar.
So many emotions,
    so many thoughts.
You confound me, Lord,
    each and every day.
Even your birth
    challenges me,
    asks me questions,
    pushes me forward.
I have no choice but to face the challenge,
    hear the questions
    and follow those shepherds
    to that stable
    of so long ago.

Amen.

What news have you ever been given that you've been unable to keep to yourself?

What's the most amazing thing you've ever seen, something that really changed your life?

This time of year is all about the birth of Jesus, no matter what advertising and marketing executives would have us believe. If this is the case, how excited do you sound when you actually talk about what Christmas means to you?

This is a pivotal moment. Only two people have so far seen Jesus, looked into his eyes, been amazed by what was unfolding in front of them – an event they were an intrinsic part of. Now though, that changes. These men arrive, and rough they are too. Probably smelling a bit ripe from being with the sheep day and night. They're a bit buzzed, excited, keep garbling on about some angels or something, won't shut up, and their language is probably just that little bit earthy. But these are real people, God's people, the people he loves. And it is these people who first see Jesus. The first humans to witness this amazing event as outsiders to what was going on. These wild, tough men are presented with the reality of what the angels told them. And there they witness their God made man, as a helpless child bathed in the love of his parents. How can this life, this story, ever fail to stop us in our tracks, amaze us, stun us, fill us with awe?

24 December
Christmas Eve

John 1:1-5
In the beginning was the one who is called the Word. The Word was with God and was truly God. From the very beginning the Word was with God. And with this Word, God created all things. Nothing was made without the Word. Everything that was created received its life from him, and his life gave light to everyone. The light keeps shining in the dark, and the darkness has never put it out.

Tomorrow, Lord,
    I'll be celebrating your birth.
I'll be enjoying a day
    dedicated to your arrival on earth
    which changed it for ever.

It's dressed up a bit, Lord.
Lots of other things going on.
Presents, food,
    family, laughter,
    snacks, telly, games . . .
But as all those things happen,
    as I experience every bit about Christmas
    that I've spent my life getting excited about,
    I want to remember that the reason for it all,

the reason for the celebration,
is you.

Now that's something to celebrate, Lord!
You turning up and flipping the world on its head.
You being born in the most outlandish of ways
    into a world that just didn't know
    how desperately it needed to meet you
    face to face.
You living the life you did,
    down here,
    with us,
    up close and personal.

You came to us,
    demonstrated exactly what love really meant,
    how a life should be led,
    and made us understand at long last
    what was meant by that simple word,
    'Hope'.

Amen.

Look back over the last month. What have you learned about yourself, about your beliefs, about what Christmas really means to you?

How real does the birth of Jesus now seem to you? Is it still something distant, camouflaged by years of school plays and television specials, or is it right in front of you, so close you can't ignore it?

Tomorrow it's Christmas Day and hopefully you're looking forward to it. Advent is now coming to an end as the very thing we've been thinking about is celebrated – the birth of Jesus. Looking back over Advent, it's probably been a time both strange and wonderful. Lots to look forward to and at the same time lots to plan and worry about and organise. Lots to smile about and at the same time lots to make you think, to question what is going on, what the real meaning behind all the celebrations really is. But that's what Advent is about. It's about preparing ourselves for the real purpose of Christmas, getting ourselves ready for what it really means to us today. The reality of Christmas, of Jesus' birth can be a shocking one. That this man was the Word of God and yet was born into our world, lived as we too live, though also as God. It's too much to comprehend at times, heads spin, brains shut down, it's too big, too huge for us to deal with. But the flip side is that what really happened, that simple act of God becoming man, being born to Mary and growing, learning, living, loving, with his people, is something so breathtakingly beautiful that we have no choice but to stand in awe. The light shines in the darkness and we see it and grin because this is the most amazing story ever told, ever to have happened, and if we want we can be a part of it!

25 December
Christmas Day

Luke 2:8-11
That night in the fields near Bethlehem some shepherds were guarding their sheep. All at once an angel came down to them from the Lord, and the brightness of the Lord's glory flashed around them. The shepherds were frightened. But the angel said, 'Don't be afraid! I have good news for you, which will make everyone happy. This very day in King David's home town a Saviour was born for you. He is Christ the Lord.

Lord!
This is it!
Christmas Day!
Fantastic!
I'm so excited – it's like being 5 all over again.
And you know what?
It just doesn't matter!

I'm going to spend every minute of today
    enjoying absolutely everything.
From the presents
    to the pudding
    to just sitting around
    and smiling at my friends and family.

25 DECEMBER

This is a short prayer, Lord,
    because I've got to get going -
    things to open, stuff to eat . . .
But I just want you to know
    that I'm eternally grateful
    for your birth
    and for what it brought
    and meant
    to this world
    and to me.

Amen.

What's the best part of today? What are you really looking forward to?

If this is what celebrating Jesus' birth makes you feel like, how are you going to let this feeling infiltrate the rest of your life?

A newborn child, a Saviour. It's all change for the world. What changes do you need to make to yourself, your life, your world?

This is it! This is really it! Jesus has been born and it's a time to go totally crazy with this amazing news! Forget the presents and pudding and Christmas crackers and bad jokes told by aunties you don't know that well; this is where it's at! How much more of a reason do you need to really celebrate? But stop. Why are you celebrating? OK, so Jesus was the Son of God, but so what? What does that mean to you today, tomorrow, for the rest of your life? Have a look at the way Jesus was born, all that is recorded to have happened, and you'll see that when God gets really involved, people get messed around, challenged, pushed, disrupted. So think on this as you celebrate what today is really about – where is the evidence of God's disruptive presence in your life? And if you can't see it, why should anyone else be able to?

31 December
New Year's Eve

Acts 5:29-31
Peter and the apostles replied, 'We don't obey people. We obey God. You killed Jesus by nailing him to a cross. But the God our ancestors worshipped raised him to life and made him our Leader and Saviour. Then God gave him a place at his right side, so that the people of Israel would turn back to him and be forgiven.

Getting involved, Lord.
That's scary.
And as another New Year approaches,
    I can't help but wonder what I'll be getting involved in.

New starts are exciting
    and frightening.
Who knows what I'll be doing in six months' time?
Who knows how I'll have changed,
    what I'll be thinking,
    what new people I'll have met,
    what new places I'll have seen?

I'm stunned by how open
    my future is,
    by how much freedom I really do have.
I can achieve so much,

do so much,
see so much.
But I don't want to do this alone, Lord.
This isn't just about me,
   it's about what I can do with your help,
   your guidance.
Afterall, there's little point in setting out
   on an adventure
   without at least some advice
   on what it's going to be like,
   what I might encounter.
Thing is,
   with you, Lord,
   I've got my own guide.

Stay by my side, Lord,
   as a new trail opens
   in my life.

Amen.

Do you want an easy life where everything is given to you on a silver platter, where money comes easy and you don't have to do much? Or do you want a life with an element of risk, where the rewards are huge but so are the costs? Where your all will be demanded and more? Where reaching the summit of one mountain brings you face-to-face with another larger mountain? Your choice. Your freedom. Your life.

31 DECEMBER

If the reality of the birth of Jesus means anything to us today, if it is to affect our lives, infect our minds, then we have no other option but to have faith and follow. But it's not easy. Why though, is this the case? All Jesus asks of us is to love each other as we would want to be loved, to love God with everything that we are, and to follow him. That's it in a nutshell. So why do we complain and moan and ignore what we're supposed to do? Christmas is a good example of why we're like this. It's a time when the emphasis is on bright lights, tasty food, comfort, rest. It's about taking it easy, having fun, eating a bit too much, giving and getting presents. And all this distracts us so easily. It's an easy life, a life we want to lead. Getting up and doing something takes effort, it requires something of us, something deep and personal. It costs us to live like Jesus. There are standards; we can't see injustice simply continue. We have to stand up for those who are wronged, free those who are persecuted. And sometimes doing this, doing what is right and good, will cost us our time, our freedom, our lives. But then Jesus never said that the right way was the easy way and demonstrated the point to full effect by what he did with his life here on earth. We just need to decide whether we want to stay sitting on the sofa, living it easy, or instead get up and walk out of the door and get involved in the world in the same way Jesus would and does through us.

1 January
New Year's Day

John 10:10
I came so that everyone would have life, and have it fully.

Lord,
   it's the new year,
   that time when everything is fresh,
   it's a new start,
   a new beginning.

I feel like I've woken up to a brand new day
   and this time everything is fresh, different.
Thinking my way through Advent,
   about what your birth really meant,
   about what it really means,
   has given me a whole new perspective
   on what's going on.

Your story, Lord,
   your life,
   feels so fresh in my mind.
I think perhaps I got bored with some of it –
   heard it all before,
   that kind of thing.

But looking at it,
    glancing at the wider picture,
    new ideas,
    new thoughts and questions,
    and the reality of you
    and what you really are
    has stopped me in my tracks.

Lord,
    in this fresh, new understanding of you,
    as I stand at the door to a new year in my life,
    help me
    to experience a new birth
    of all that I am,
    all that you want me to be
    and all that we can be
    together.

Amen.

New Year, new start. What changes are you planning to make this year?

Think of something you want to achieve over the next twelve months. Plan it and do it – don't make excuses.

Where do you see your relationship with God twelve months from now? How are you going to achieve that?

ADVERTS AND ADVENT

New life. New start. Fresh beginning. Time to make a real difference. The start of something amazing. New rules. New ideals. That's what Advent and Christmas are all about. It's a time of hope, of opportunity, of you, of God, of where it all goes, what it all means, what you can do about it, what God can do with you. New Year. New life. New start. With God. With you.